Basic Spanish for Travelers

by

Copyright ©2005 by Language 9-1-1, Inc.
All rights reserved.
Basic Spanish for Travelers
Published by Language 9-1-1 in Palm Beach Gardens, FL

Library of Congress Cataloging-in-Publication Data

Language 9-1-1, Inc.
    Basic spanish for travelers / by Language 9-1-1, Inc.
    ISBN 1-933451-02-5

CONTENTS

AUDIO CD TRACK LIST

Track #	Track Title

INTRODUCTION

Before you begin, please be aware of the following:

Spoken by some 300 million people, Spanish is the most popular of the Romance languages. It is the official language of Spain, Puerto Rico, and most Latin American countries. There are between 15 and 20 million Spanish-speaking people residing in the United States.

The Spanish spoken in Spain is called Castillian Spanish. The Spanish of Latin America is called American Spanish. The two types of Spanish are very similar with the exception of a few basic sounds. Spaniards and Latin Americans have no problem understanding each other. The Spanish presented in this program is that of Latin America.

SPANISH PRONUNCIATION

BEGIN THE CD NOW

Spanish is relatively easy to pronounce for English-speaking people, due primarily to the fact that written Spanish closely reflects the sounds of spoken Spanish. There are two primary dialects: Castillian Spanish of Spain and American Spanish spoken in Latin America. Within Latin America there are at least five major variations. Nonetheless, all dialects and variations of Spanish are mutually intelligible. The dialect in this program is American Spanish. The native speaker, Lucy, is from Bogotá, Colombia.

In Spanish only one syllable can be stressed in a word. The vowels (a, e, i, o, u) are pure and do not change.

HINTS FOR BETTER SPANISH PRONUNCIATION

1. The letter "ñ" sounds like the "ni" in the English word onion.
   Examples: leña, año, señor

2. The double "ll" has no "l" sound. It sounds like the "y" in the English word yeah.
   Examples: caballo, calle, llevar

3. An accent mark indicates that a syllable should be stressed.
   Examples: apagó, pálido, policía

4. The letter "j" is pronounced like an English "h".
   Examples: José, Jacinto, Alajuela

5. The letter "g" when followed by "e" or "i" is also pronounced like an English "h".
   Examples: general, alergia, ginebra

6. The double "rr" and the initial "r" of a word are always trilled.
   Examples: carro, Roberto, rumor, ocurrió

7. The letter "h" is silent.
   Examples: hola, ahora, hielo

PHONETIC APPROXIMATIONS

Remember: The phonetic approximations only approximate the sounds of Spanish. Use them to assist you with the pronunciation when necessary. When you read the approximations in English you will be understood in Spanish, although you may sound somewhat "foreign." Also, notice that in the phonetic approximations, syllables written in the upper case should be stressed. Example: BWAY-nohs. Hyphens separate syllables and slash marks separate words. A double rr indicates a trilled r. A plus sign indicates that two sounds are to be fused together. Example: BEE+ENN.

SECTION 1: GREETINGS AND GOODBYES (CD Tracks 5 & 6)

	English	Spanish	Phonetic Approximations
1.	Mister or Sir.	Señor.	say-NYOR
2.	Mrs. or Ma'am.	Señora.	say-NYOH-rah
3.	Miss.	Señorita.	say-nyoh-REE-tah
4.	Good day. *OR* Good morning.	Buenos días.	BWAY-nose / DEE-ahs
5.	Good afternoon.	Buenas tardes.	BWAY-nahs / TAR-days
6.	Good evening. *OR* Good night.	Buenas noches.	BWAY-nahs / NOH-chays
7.	Hello.	Hola.	OH-lah
8.	Welcome.	Bienvenido.	bee+enn-vay-NEE-doh
9.	Goodbye.	Adiós.	ah-DEE+OHS
10.	Until later.	Hasta luego.	AHS-tah / LWAY-goh
11.	Until tomorrow.	Hasta mañana.	AHS-tah / mah-NYAH-nah
12.	Have a good trip.	Buen viaje.	BWANE / BEE+AH-hay
13.	How are you?*	¿Cómo está?	KOH-moh / ess-TAH
14.	Very well.	Muy bien.	MWEE / BEE+ENN
15.	And you?	¿Y usted?	EE / oose-TED

*NOTE: This is a serious question that inquires as to the state of a person.

SECTION 2: ETIQUETTE AND SOCIAL NICETIES (CD Tracks 7 & 8)

	English	Spanish	Phonetic Approximations
1.	Yes.	Sí.	SEE
2.	No.	No.	NOH
3.	Excuse me. (when leaving the table)	Con permiso.	CONE / pair-MEE-soh
4.	Excuse me. (when bumping into someone)	Perdóneme.	pair-DOH-nay-may
5.	Please.	Por favor.	POR / fah-VOHR
6.	Thank you.	Gracias.	GRAH-see+ahs
7.	You're welcome.	De nada.	day / NAH-dah
8.	I'm sorry.	Lo siento.	loh / SEE+ENN-toh
9.	Come in.	Pase.	PAH-say
10.	Sit down.	Siéntese.	SEE+ENN-tay-say
11.	May I?	¿Me permite?	MAY / pair-MEE-tay
12.	Allow me.	Permítame.	pair-MEE-tah-may
13.	Okay.	Está bien.	ess-TAH / BEE+ENN
14.	Good luck.	Buena suerte.	BWAY-nah / SWEAR-tay
15.	Enjoy your meal.	Buen provecho.	BWANE / proh-VAY-choh
16.	Cheers!	¡Salud!	sah-LEWD
17.	God bless you! (after a sneeze)	¡Salud!	sah-LEWD

SECTION 3: INTRODUCTIONS AND SELF-IDENTIFICATION (CD Tracks 9 & 10)

English	Spanish	Phonetic Approximations
1. My name is __(name)__ .	Mi nombre es __(name)__ .	mee / NOME-bray / ess / ____
2. What is your name?	¿Cuál es su nombre?	KWAL / ess / soo / NOME-bray
3. I'm __(name, title, or position)__ .	Soy __(name, title, or position)__ .	SOY / ____
4. I work for __(company name)__ .	Trabajo para __(company name)__ .	trah-BAH-hoh / PAH-rah / ____
5. I'm from __(city, state, or country)__ .	Soy de __(city, state, or country)__ .	SOY / day / ____
6. I am from the United States.	Soy de los Estados Unidos.*	SOY / day / lohs / ess-TAH-dohs / oo-NEE-dohs
7. My wife, __(wife's name)__ .	Mi esposa, __(wife's name)__ .	mee / ess-POH-sah / ____
8. My husband, __(husband's name)__ .	Mi esposo, __(husband's name)__ .	mee / ess-POH-soh / ____
9. My colleague, __(name)__ .	Mi colega, __(name)__ .	mee / koh-LAY-gah / ____
10. My friend, __(name)__ .	Mi amigo, __(name)__ . (if friend is male) Mi amiga, __(name)__ . (if friend is female)	mee / ah-MEE-goh / ____ mee / ah-MEE-gah / ____
11. Nice to meet you.	Mucho gusto.	MOO-choh / GOOSE-toh
12. The pleasure is mine.	El gusto es mío.	ell / GOOSE-toh / ess / MEE-oh

***NOTE:** The United States is often abbreviated on signs and documents as EEUU or EU.

SECTION 4: NUMBERS (CD Tracks 11 & 12)

	English	Spanish	Phonetic Approximations
0.	zero	cero	SAY-roh
1.	one	uno	OO-noh
2.	two	dos	DOHS
3.	three	tres	TRACE
4.	four	cuatro	KWAH-troh
5.	five	cinco	SEEN-koh
6.	six	seis	SACE
7.	seven	siete	SEE+AY-tay
8.	eight	ocho	OH-choh
9.	nine	nueve	NWAY-vay
10.	ten	diez	DEE+ESS
11.	eleven	once	OHN-say
12.	twelve	doce	DOH-say
13.	thirteen	trece	TRAY-say
14.	fourteen	catorce	kah-TOR-say
15.	fifteen	quince	KEEN-say
16.	sixteen	diez y seis	DEE+ESS / ee / SACE
17.	seventeen	diez y siete	DEE+ESS / ee / SEE+AY-tay

SECTION 4: NUMBERS (CONTINUED)

18.	eighteen	diez y ocho	DEE+ESS / ee / OH-choh
19.	nineteen	diez y nueve	DEE+ESS / ee / NWAY-vay
20.	twenty	veinte	VAIN-tay
21.	twenty-one	veinte y uno	VAIN-tay / ee / OO-noh
22.	twenty-two	veinte y dos	VAIN-tay / ee / DOHS
23.	twenty-three	veinte y tres	VAIN-tay / ee / TRACE
24.	twenty-four	veinte y cuatro	VAIN-tay / ee / KWAH-troh
25.	twenty-five	veinte y cinco	VAIN-tay / ee / SEEN-koh
26.	twenty-six	veinte y seis	VAIN-tay / ee / SACE
27.	twenty-seven	veinte y siete	VAIN-tay / ee / SEE+AY-tay
28.	twenty-eight	veinte y ocho	VAIN-tay / ee / OH-choh
29.	twenty-nine	veinte y nueve	VAIN-tay / ee / NWAY-vay
30.	thirty	treinta	TRAIN-tah
31.	thirty-one	treinta y uno	TRAIN-tah / ee / OO-noh
32.	thirty-two	treinta y dos etc...etc...etc...	TRAIN-tah / ee / DOHS

NOTE: To count from 31-99, the Spanish numbering system links two digit numbers and one digit numbers with the word *y*, which means "and." For example, the number 55 is rendered by saying fifty AND five, or *cincuenta y cinco*. Seventy-eight, for instance, is "seventy AND eight," or *setenta y ocho*.

SECTION 4: NUMBERS (CONTINUED)

40.	forty	cuarenta	kwah-REN-tah
41.	forty-one	cuarenta y uno etc...etc...etc...	kwah-REN-tah / ee / OO-noh
50.	fifty	cincuenta	seen-KWEN-tah
60.	sixty	sesenta	say-SEN-tah
70.	seventy	setenta	say-TEN-tah
80.	eighty	ochenta	oh-CHEN-tah
90.	ninety	noventa	noh-VEN-tah
100.	one hundred	cien	SEE+ENN
101.	one hundred and one	ciento uno	SEE+ENN-toh / OO-noh
102.	one hundred and two	ciento dos etc...etc...etc...	SEE+ENN-toh / DOHS
200.	two hundred	doscientos	dohs-SEE+ENN-tohs
300.	three hundred	trescientos	trace-SEE+ENN-tohs
400.	four hundred	cuatrocientos	kwah-troh-SEE+ENN-tohs
500.	five hundred	quinientos	kee-NYENN-tohs
600.	six hundred	seiscientos	sace-SEE+ENN-tohs
700.	seven hundred	setecientos	say-tay-SEE+ENN-tohs
800.	eight hundred	ochocientos	oh-choh-SEE+ENN-tohs
900.	nine hundred	novecientos	noh-vay-SEE+ENN-tohs
1,000.	one thousand	mil	MEAL
2,000.	two thousand	dos mil etc...etc...etc...	DOHS / MEAL

SECTION 5: COMPLIMENTS, LIKES, AND DISLIKES (CD Tracks 13 & 14)

	English	Spanish	Phonetic Approximations
1.	Magnificent.	Magnífico.	mahg-NEE-fee-koh
2.	Pretty. (people and things)	Bonito.	boh-NEE-toh
3.	Delicious. (food and drink)	Delicioso.	day-lee-SEE+OH-soh
4.	It's good.	Es bueno.	ess / BWAY-noh
5.	I like it. (point to object)	Me gusta.	may / GOOSE-tah
6.	I like _(supply item)_ .	Me gusta _(supply item)_ .	may / GOOSE-tah / _____
7.	I don't like it. (point to object)	No me gusta.	NOH / may / GOOSE-tah
8.	I don't like _(supply item)_ .	No me gusta _(supply item)_ .	NOH / may / GOOSE-tah / _____
9.	How wonderful!	¡Qué bien!	KAY / BEE+ENN
10.	Good idea!	¡Buena idea!	BWAY-nah / ee-DAY-ah
11.	Well done!	¡Bien hecho!	BEE+ENN / AY-choh
12.	Well said!	¡Bien dicho!	BEE+ENN / DEE-choh
13.	You are very kind.	Usted es muy amable.	oose-TED / ess / MWEE / ah-MAH-blay
14.	You speak English very well.	Usted habla inglés muy bien.	oose-TED / AH-blah / een-GLAYS / MWEE / BEE+ENN

NOTE: One of the simplest and most effective ways to impress your counterpart(s) in Spanish-speaking countries is to compliment the local beer or a national food dish. Also, try complimenting a local product, a city monument, a natural attraction, the countryside, the weather, or anything else that comes to mind.

SECTION 6: ORDERING FOOD AND DRINK (CD Tracks 15 & 16)

English	Spanish	Phonetic Approximations
1. The menu, please.	El menú, por favor.	ell / may-NOO / POR / fah-VOR
2. I want (supply food or drink) .	Deseo (supply food or drink) .	day-SAY-oh / _____
3. I want this. (point to food on menu)	Deseo esto. (point to food on menu)	day-SAY-oh / ESS-toh
4. Do you have (supply food or drink) ?	¿Hay (supply food or drink) ?	eye / _____
5. Without ice.	Sin hielo.	SEEN / YEAH-loh
6. With ice.	Con hielo.	CONE / YEAH-loh
7. Nothing else, thank you.	Nada más, gracias.	NAH-dah / MAHS / GRAH-see+ahs
8. The bill, please.	La cuenta, por favor.	lah / KWEN-tah / POR / fah-VOR
9. Do you accept (name of credit card) ?	¿Acepta (name of credit card) ?	ah-SAYP-tah / _____

NOTE: To effectively use the phrases above, consult the "Food Request List" and "Menu Reader" on pages 19 and 20.

SECTION 7: GETTING PLACES IN A TAXI (CD Tracks 17 & 18)

English	Spanish	Phonetic Approximations
1. Where are the taxis?	¿Dónde están los taxis?	DOAN-day / ess-TAHN / lohs / TALK-sees
2. I need a taxi.	Necesito un taxi.	nay-say-SEE-toh / oon / TALK-see
3. Taxi!	¡Taxi!	TALK-see
4. I'm going to (supply destination).	Voy a (supply destination).	VOY / ah / _____
5. I'm going to the train station.	Voy a la estación del tren.	VOY / ah / lah / ess-tah-SEE+OHN / dell / TRENN
5. I'm going to the airport.	Voy al aeropuerto.	VOY / all / ah+ay-row-PWEAR-toh
6. I'm going downtown.	Voy al centro.	VOY / all / SEN-troh
7. I'm going to the Hotel (name of hotel).	Voy al Hotel (name of hotel).	VOY / all / oh-TELL / _____.
8. I'm going to this address, please. (Hand driver written address.)	Voy a esta dirección, por favor.	VOY / ah / ESS-tah / dee-wreck-SEE+OWN / POR / fah-VOHR
9. What's the fare?	¿Cuánto cuesta?	KWAN-toh / KWAYS-tah

SECTION 8: HOTEL NEEDS (CD Tracks 19 & 20)

English	Spanish	Phonetic Approximations
1. I have a reservation.	Tengo reservación.	TEN-goh / rray-sair-vah-SEE+OWN
2. My name is (name).	Mi nombre es (name).	MEE / NOME-bray / ess / _____
3. I need a single room.	Necesito habitación sencilla.	nay-say-SEE-toh / ah-bee-tah-SEE+OWN / sen-SEE-yah
4. I need a double room.	Necesito habitación doble.	nay-say-SEE-toh / ah-bee-tah-SEE+OWN / DOH-blay
5. I am staying (number) days.	Me quedo (number) días.	may / KAY-doh / _____ / DEE-ahs
6. How much per day?	¿Cuánto por día?	KWAN-toh / por / DEE-ah
7. I need (supply item).	Necesito (supply item).	nay-say-SEE-toh / _____
8. My key, please.	Mi llave, por favor.	mee / YAH-vay / POR / fah-VOR
9. My room number is (room no.).	Mi número de habitación es (room no.).	mee / NOO-may-row / day / ah-bee-tah-SEE+OWN / ess / _____
10. Is there laundry service?	¿Hay servicio de lavandería?	eye / sair-VEE-see+oh / day / lah-vahn-day-REE-ah
11. Is there a bar near here?	¿Hay un bar cerca de aquí?	eye / oon / BAR / SAIR-kah / day / ah-KEE
12. Is there a restaurant near here?	¿Hay un restaurante cerca de aquí?	eye / oon / rrays-tah+oo-RAHN-tay / SAIR-kah / day / ah-KEE

SECTION 9: COMMUNICATION STRATEGIES (CD Tracks 21 & 22)

	English	Spanish	Phonetic Approximations
1.	Do you speak English?	¿Habla inglés?	AH-blah / een-GLAYS
2.	I understand.	Entiendo.	enn-TEE+ENN-doh
3.	I don't understand.	No entiendo.	NOH / enn-TEE+ENN-doh
4.	Do you understand me?	¿Me entiende?	MAY / enn-TEE+ENN-day
5.	Say it again.	Repítalo.	rray-PEE-tah-loh
6.	Speak slowly.	Hable despacio.	AH-blay / days-PAH-see+oh
7.	Write it, please.	Escríbalo, por favor.	ess-KREE-bah-loh / POR / fah-VOR
8.	I need an interpreter.	Necesito un intérprete.	nay-say-SEE-toh / oon / een-TAIR-pray-tay
9.	I don't speak Spanish.	No hablo español.	NOH / AH-bloh / ess-pah-NYOL
10.	You speak English very well.	Usted habla inglés muy bien.	oose-TED / AH-blah / een-GLAYS / MWEE / BEE+ENN

NOTE: Once you have mastered the Spanish in this program, some Spanish-speaking people may assume that you are fluent in their language. Therefore, we have included these communication strategies not only to facilitate communication, but also to allow you to indicate that your knowledge of Spanish is very limited.

SECTION 10: SHOPPING (CD Tracks 23 & 24)

English	Spanish	Phonetic Approximations
1. How much does it cost? (point to object)	¿Cuánto cuesta?	KWAN-toh / KWAYS-tah
2. That's a lot.*	Es mucho.	ess / MOO-choh
3. No, thanks.	No, gracias.	NOH / GRAH-see+ahs
4. I'm just looking.	Estoy mirando, nada más.	ess-TOY/mee-RAHN-doh/NAH-dah/MAHS
5. I want (supply item).	Deseo (supply item).	day-SAY-oh / _____
6. Show me that, please. (point to object)	Muéstreme eso, por favor.	MWAYS-tray-may / AY-soh / POR / fah-VOR
7. I want this, please. (point to or hold up object)	Deseo esto, por favor.	day-SAY-oh / ESS-toh / POR / fah-VOR
8. I'll take it.	Lo llevo.	LOH / YEAH-voh
9. Do you accept (name of credit card) ?	¿Acepta (name of credit card) ?	ah-SAYP-tah / _____

*NOTE: Bargaining is fun, but is conducted mainly in open-air markets. Be aware that most stores have fixed prices.

REMEMBER: When traveling in a foreign country it is always a good idea to carry a small bilingual pocket dictionary for emergency purposes. Line #4 above, for example, can be very effective in shopping if you have such a dictionary with you.

SECTION 11: EMERGENCIES (CD Tracks 25 & 26)

	English	Spanish	Phonetic Approximations
1.	I need help.	Necesito ayuda.	nay-say-SEE-toh / ah-YOU-dah
2.	I need the police.	Necesito la policía.	nay-say-SEE-toh / lah / poh-lee-SEE-ah
3.	I need a doctor.	Necesito un doctor.	nay-say-SEE-toh / oon / doak-TOR
4.	I need a dentist.	Necesito un dentista.	nay-say-SEE-toh / oon / den-TEES-tah
5.	I need an interpreter.	Necesito un intérprete.	nay-say-SEE-toh / oon / een-TEAR-pray-tay
6.	I need a bathroom.	Necesito un baño.	nay-say-SEE-toh / oon / BAH-nyoh
7.	I don't feel well.	Me siento mal.	may / SEE+ENN-toh / mall
8.	I'm sick.	Estoy enfermo.	ess-TOY / enn-FAIR-moh
9.	Take me to a pharmacy.	Lléveme a una farmacia.	YEAH-vay-may / ah / OO-nah / far-MAH-see+ah
10.	I need a telephone.	Necesito hablar por teléfono.	nay-say-SEE-toh / ah-BLAHR / por / tay-LAY-foh-noh
11.	I want to make a call to the U.S.	Deseo llamar a los Estados Unidos.	day-SAY-oh /yah-MAR / ah / lohs / ess-TAH-dohs / oo-NEE-dohs
12.	The number is _(phone no.)_ .	El número es _(phone no.)_ .	ell / NOO-may-roh / ess / _____

SECTION 12: TELEPHONE ETIQUETTE

English	Spanish	Phonetic Approximations

Part A: Making an International Call (CD Tracks 27 & 28)

English	Spanish	Phonetic Approximations
1. I need to speak with the international operator.	Necesito hablar con la operadora internacional.	nay-say-SEE-toh / ah-BLAR / cone / lah / oh-pay-rah-DOH-rah / een-tair-nah-SEE+OH-nahl
2. I need to make a long distance call.	Necesito hacer una llamada de larga distancia.	nay-say-SEE-toh / ah-SAIR / OO-nah / yah-MAH-dah / day / LAR-gah / dees-TAHN-see+ah
3. I need to call the U.S.	Necesito llamar a los Estados Unidos.	nay-say-SEE-toh / yah-MAR / ah / lohs / ess-TAH-dohs / oo-NEE-dohs
4. The number is (give number) .	El número es (give number) .	ell / NOO-may-roh / ess / _____
5. Collect, please.	Por cobrar, por favor.	POR / koh-BRAR / POR / fah-VOR
6. My name is (your name) .	Mi nombre es (your name) .	MEE / NOME-bray / ess / _____
7. Calling card call, please.*	Llamada con tarjeta de llamadas, por favor.	yah-MAH-dah / cone / tar-HAY-tah / day / yah-MAH-dahs / POR / fah-VOR
8. My card number is (give number) .	El número de mi tarjeta es (give number) .	ell / NOO-may-roh / day / mee / tar-HAY-tah / ess / _____

SECTION 12: TELEPHONE ETIQUETTE (CONTINUED)

English	Spanish	Phonetic Approximations

Part B: Making a Local Call (CD Tracks 29 & 30)

1. Is (name) there?
   ¿Está (name) ?
   ess-TAH / _____

2. May I speak with (name) ?
   ¿Puedo hablar con (name) ?
   PWAY-doh / ah-BLAR / cone / _____

3. This is (name) .
   Habla (name) .
   AH-blah / _____

4. Is there anyone there who speaks English?
   ¿Hay alguien allí que hable inglés?
   eye / all-GEE+ENN / ah-YEE / kay / AH-blay / een-GLAYS

5. Please tell him/her to call (name) .
   Por favor, dígale que llame a (name) .
   POR / fah-VOR / DEE-gah-lay / kay / YAH-may / ah / _____

6. The number is (number) .
   El número es (number) .
   ell / NOO-may-roh / ess / _____

7. Thank you, goodbye.
   Gracias, hasta luego.
   GRAH-see+ahs / AHS-tah / LWAY-goh

Part C: Receiving a Call (CD Tracks 31 & 32)

1. Hello.
   Diga.
   DEE-gah

2. Who is speaking, please?
   ¿Quién habla, por favor?
   KEE+ENN / AH-blah / POR / fah-VOR

3. This is (name) .
   Habla (name) .
   AH-blah / _____

4. I don't speak Spanish.
   No hablo español.
   NOH / AH-bloh / ess-pah-NYOHL

SECTION 13: COMMON FIRST AND LAST NAMES (CD Track 33)

1. Juan Acosta
2. José Álvarez
3. Jaime Botero
4. Pedro Bravo
5. Francisco Bernal
6. Jorge Caballero
7. Carlos Cantú
8. Mauricio Chávez
9. Oscar Contreras
10. Alberto Dávila
11. Miguel Díaz
12. César Domínguez
13. Julio Escobar
14. Rafael Fernández
15. Ricardo Flores
16. Guillermo Fuentes
17. Pablo Galván

18. Luis García
19. Eduardo Garza
20. Enrique Gaviria
21. Humberto Gómez
22. Manuel González
23. Sergio Gutiérrez
24. Rodrigo Hernández
25. Roberto Huertas
26. Diana Jaramillo
27. Marcela León
28. Teresa López
29. Sandra Martínez
30. Angélica Mendoza
31. Clara Menéndez
32. Patricia Morales
33. Beatriz Muñoz
34. Cristina Orozco

35. Liliana Ortiz
36. Olga Pacheco
37. Lucía Peña
38. María Pérez
39. Yolanda Quintero
40. Alicia Ramírez
41. Adriana Rodríguez
42. Carmen Rojas
43. Guadalupe Ríos
44. Alejandra Salinas
45. Gabriela Sánchez
46. Claudia Santos
47. Silvia Torres
48. Carolina Treviño
49. Ana Vásquez
50. Laura Velasco

This is the end of the Disc.

NOTE: People's names are dear to them, and they appreciate it if you can pronounce them without undue distortion. Impress your Spanish counterpart by pronouncing his/her first and last name correctly. It will pay rich dividends!

APPENDIX A: FOOD REQUEST LIST [ENGLISH → SPANISH]

appetizer - la tapa, el aperitivo, la botana
apple - la manzana
avocado - el aguacate
bacon - el tocino
banana - la banana, el plátano
beans - los frijoles
beef - la carne (de res)
beef steak - el bistec
beer - la cerveza
beverage - la bebida
bill - la cuenta, la factura
black - negro(a)
bowl - el plato hondo
bread - el pan
breakfast - el desayuno
butter - la mantequilla
cabbage - la col, el repollo
cake - la torta, el pastel
cantaloupe - el melón
caramel custard - el flan
carrot - la zanahoria
cereals - los cereales
champagne - la champán
cheese - el queso
chicken - el pollo
chef - el cocinero
cold - frío, helado
cottage cheese - el requesón, el queso cottage
crab - el cangrejo
cucumber - el pepino
cup - la taza
cup of coffee (tea) - la taza de café (té)
delicious - sabroso, delicioso
dessert - el postre
dining room - el comedor
dinner - la comida
dish - el plato
dried meat - la machaca
drink - la bebida
egg - el huevo
entree - la entrada
fish - el pescado
food - los comestibles, los alimentos, la comida
fork - el tenedor
fried - frito(a)
fruit - la fruta
fruit and wine drink - la sangría
fruit cocktail - el coctel de frutas
glass - el vaso
glass of water - el vaso de agua

grape - la uva
grapefruit - la toronja
green - verde
green beans - las judías verdes
grilled - a la parrilla
ham - el jamón
hamburger - la hamburguesa
honey - la miel
hot - caliente
hot peppers - los chiles
ice cream - el helado
jelly - la mermelada
juice - el jugo
ketchup - el catsup, la salsa de tomate
knife - el cuchillo
lamb - el cordero
lemonade - la limonada
lettuce - la lechuga
lime - el limón
lobster – la langosta
lunch – el almuerzo
mayonnaise - la mayonesa
meat - la carne
medium - término medio
medium rare - medio crudo
menu – el menú
mexican style - a la mexicana
milk - la leche
milkshake - la leche malteada
mineral water – el agua mineral
mushroom - el hongo, champiñón
mustard - la mostaza
nuts - las nueces
oatmeal - la avena
omelet - la tortilla española
orange - la naranja
order - el pedido
pasta - las pastas
peanut butter - la mantequilla de cacahuete (de maní)
peas - los guisantes, los chícharos
pepper - la pimienta
pepper shaker - el pimentero
pineapple - la piña
plate - el plato
pork - el cerdo, el puerco
pork chop - la chuleta de cerdo
potato - la papa
preference (of) - al gusto
ranch style - rancheros
red - rojo(a)
reservation - la reservación
restaurant - el restaurante

rice - el arroz
rice pudding - el arroz con leche
salad - la ensalada
salad dressing - el aderezo para ensalada
salt - la sal
salt shaker - el salero
sausage - la salchicha
seafood - los mariscos
shellfish - el marisco
shrimp - los camarones
shrimp cocktail - el coctel de camarones
silverware - los cubiertos
soft drinks - los refrescos, las gaseosas
soft taco - taco
soup - la sopa
soup (cold, made of tomatoes, cucumbers, & onions) - el gazpacho
spaghetti - los espaguetis
spanish rice - la paella
spinach - las espinacas
spoon - la cuchara
stuffed - relleno
sugar - el azúcar
straw - el popote, el pitillo
strawberry - la fresa
supper - la cena
sweet - dulce
syrup - la miel de maple
table - la mesa
tip - la propina
toasted - tostado
tomato - el tomate
tray - la bandeja
trout - trucha
tuna - el atún
turkey - el pavo
vegetables - las legumbres, los vegetales, las verduras
waiter - el camarero, el mesero
waitress - la camarera, la mesera
well-done - bien cocido
white bread - el pan blanco
whole wheat bread - el pan integral
wine - el vino
wine (blush) – el vino rosado
wine (red) – el vino tinto
wine (white) – el vino blanco
wine glass - la copa
wine list - la lista de vinos
yogurt - el yogur

APPENDIX B: MENU READER [SPANISH → ENGLISH]

agua mineral - mineral water
aguacate - avocado
alimentos - food
a la mexicana - mexican style
a la parrilla - grilled
al gusto - the way you like it
almuerzo - lunch
aperitivo - appetizer
arroz - rice
arroz con leche - rice pudding
atún - tuna
avena - oatmeal
azúcar - sugar
bandeja - tray
bebida - drink, beverage
bien cocido - well done
bistec - beef steak
botana - appetizer
caliente - hot
camarero(a) - waiter; waitress
camarones - shrimp
cangrejo - crab
catsup - ketchup
carne (de res) - beef, meat
cena - supper
cerdo - pork
cereales - cereals
cerveza - beer
champán - champagne
champiñón - mushroom
chícharos – peas
chiles - hot peppers
chuleta de cerdo - pork chop
cocinero - chef
coctel de camarones - shrimp
    cocktail
coctel de frutas - fruit cocktail
col - cabbage
comedor - dinning room
comestibles - food
comida - dinner, food
copa - wine glass
cordero - lamb
cubiertos - silverware
cuchara - spoon
cuchillo - knife
cuenta - bill
desayuno - breakfast
dulce - sweet
ensalada - salad
entrada - entree
espaguetis - spaghetti
espinacas - spinach
factura - bill
flan - caramel custard

fresa - strawberry
frijoles - beans
frío - cold
frito(a) - fried
fruta - fruit
gaseosas - soft drinks
gazpacho - soup (cold, made of
    tomatoes, cucumbers, &
    onions)
guisantes - peas
hamburguesa - hamburger
harina - flour
helado - cold, ice cream
hongo - mushroom
huevo - egg, omelet
jamón - ham
judías verdes - green beans
jugo - juice
langosta - lobster
leche - milk
leche malteada - milkshake
lechuga - lettuce
legumbres - vegetables
limón - lime
limonada - lemonade
lista de vinos - wine list
machaca - dried meat
maíz - corn
mantequilla - butter
mantequilla de cacahuete (de maní)
    - peanut butter
manzana - apple
mariscos - seafood, shellfish
mayonesa - mayonnaise
medio crudo - medium rare
melón - cantaloupe
menú - menu
mermelada - jelly
mesa - table
mesero(a) - waiter; waitress
miel - honey
miel de maple - syrup
mostaza - mustard
naranja - orange
negro(a) - black
nueces - nuts
paella - spanish rice
pan - bread
pan blanco - white bread
pan integral - whole wheat bread
papa - potato
pastas - pasta
pavo - turkey
pedido - order
pepino - cucumber

pescado - fish
pimienta - pepper
pimentero - pepper shaker
piña - pineapple
pitillo - straw
plátano - banana
plato - dish, plate
plato hondo - bowl
pollo - chicken
popote - straw
postre - dessert
propina - tip
puerco - pork
rancheros - ranch style
refrescos - soft drinks
requesón - cottage cheese
relleno - stuffed
repollo - cabbage
reservación - reservation
restaurante - restaurant
rojo(a) - red
queso - cheese
queso cottage - cottage cheese
sabroso - delicious
sal - salt
salchicha - sausage
salero - salt shaker
salsa de tomate - ketchup
sangría - fruit and wine drink
servilleta - napkin
sopa - soup
taco - soft taco
taza - cup
taza de café (té) - cup of coffee (tea)
tenedor - fork
término medio - medium
tocino - bacon
tomate - tomato
toronja - grapefruit
torta - cake
tortilla española - omelette
trucha - trout
uva - grape
vaso - glass
vaso de agua - glass of water
vegetales - vegetables
verde - green
verduras - vegetables
vino - wine
vino blanco - white wine
vino rosado - wine (blush)
vino tinto - red wine
yogur - yogurt
zanahoria - carrot

APPENDIX C: DATES

Months	Monate
January	enero
February	febrero
March	marzo
April	abril
May	mayo
June	junio
July	julio
August	agosto
September	septiembre
October	octubre
November	noviembre
December	diciembre

Spanish speakers report calendar dates in a slightly different manner than we do in English. The most important difference is that the day of the month is given before the name of the month (U.S. military style).

While in English we would say "January 15, 1972" (1/15/72), a Spanish speaker would say "the 15th of January of 1972" (15/1/72)

For example:	English	Spanish
	December 25, 1943	25 de diciembre de 1943 = veinte y cinco de diciembre de mil novecientos cuarenta y tres
	May 5, 1970	5 de mayo de 1970 = cinco de mayo de mil novecientos setenta

APPENDIX D: HOLIDAYS

ARGENTINA
1 January	New Year's Day
Consult Calendar	Holy Thursday
Consult Calendar	Good Friday
1 May	Labor Day
25 May	Anniversary of the May Revolution
Consult Calendar	Malvinas Day
Consult Calendar	Flag Day
9 July	Independence Day
17 August	Death of General José de San Martín
21 September	Student Day
12 October	Columbus Day
25 December	Christmas

BOLIVIA
1 January	New Year's Day
19 March	Father's Day
23 March	Sea Day
Consult Calendar	Holy Thursday
Consult Calendar	Good Friday
1 May	Labor Day
27 May	Mother's Day
6 August	Independence Day
1 November	All Saints Day
25 December	Christmas

CHILE
1 January	New Year's Day
Consult Calendar	Holy Thursday
Consult Calendar	Good Friday
1 May	Labor Day
21 May	Naval Battle of Iquique
18 September	Independence Day
19 September	Armed Forces Day
12 October	Columbus Day
1 November	All Saints Day
25 December	Christmas

COLOMBIA
1 January	New Year's Day
6 January	Epiphany
19 March	St. Joseph's Day
Consult Calendar	Holy Thursday
Consult Calendar	Good Friday
1 May	Labor day
29 June	Feast of St. Peter and St. Paul
20 July	Independence Day
7 August	Battle of Boyacá
15 August	Assumption Day
12 October	Columbus Day
1 November	All Saints Day
11 November	Independence of Cartagena
25 December	Christmas

APPENDIX D: HOLIDAYS (CONTINUED)

COSTA RICA
1 January	New Year's Day
19 March	Feast of St. Joseph
11 April	Anniversary of the Battle of Rivas against Walker
Consult Calendar	Holy Thursday
Consult Calendar	Good Friday
1 May	Labor Day
25 July	Annexation of Guanacaste to Costa Rica
29 June	Feast of St. Peter and St. Paul
2 August	Feast of our Lady of the Angels
15 September	Central American Independence Day
12 October	Columbus Day
8 December	Feast of Immaculate Conception
25 December	Christmas

DOMINICAN REPUBLIC
1 January	New Year's Day

ECUADOR
1 January	New Year's Day
Consult Calendar	Holy Thursday
Consult Calendar	Good Friday
1 May	Labor Day
24 May	Battle of Pichincha
10 August	Independence Day
9 October	Independence of Guayaquil
2 November	All Souls Day
6 December	Independence of Quito
25 December	Christmas

EL SALVADOR
1 January	New Year's Day
Consult Calendar	Easter Week
1 May	Labor Day
10 May	Mother's Day
17 June	Father's Day
1 - 5 August	August Religious Festivities
15 September	Independence Day
12 October	Columbus Day
25 December	Christmas

GUATEMALA
1 January	New Year's Day
Consult Calendar	Holy Thursday
Consult Calendar	Good Friday
1 May	Labor Day
30 June	Army Day
15 September	Independence Day
12 October	Columbus Day
20 October	Revolution Day
1 November	All Saints Day
Consult Calendar	Christmas

APPENDIX D: HOLIDAYS (CONTINUED)

HONDURAS

1 January	New Year's Day
Consult Calendar	Easter Week
14 April	Day of the Americas
1 May	Labor Day
10 September	Children's Day
15 September	Independence Day
3 October	Francisco Morazán's Birthday
12 October	Columbus Day
21 October	Armed Forces Day
25 December	Christmas

MEXICO

1 January	New Year's Day
17 January	St. Anthony's Day
5 February	Constitution Day
21 March	Benito Juárez's Birthday
Consult Calendar	Holy Thursday
Consult Calendar	Good Friday
1 May	Labor Day
5 May	Battle of Puebla Anniversary
15 August	Assumption
16 September	Independence Day
12 October	Columbus Day
1 November	All Saints Day
2 November	All Souls Day
20 November	Revolution Day
25 December	Christmas Day

NICARAGUA

1 January	New Year's Day
Consult Calendar	Easter
1 May	Labor Day
14 September	Battle of San Jacinto
15 September	Independence Day
8 December	Feast of the Immaculate Conception
25 December	Christmas

PANAMA

9 January	Day of the Martyrs
Consult Calendar	Holy Thursday
Consult Calendar	Good Friday
11 October	Anniversary of the Revolution
3 November	Independence Day
11 November	Uprising of Los Santos
28 November	Independence from Spain Day
Consult Calendar	Mother's Day
25 December	Christmas

APPENDIX D: HOLIDAYS (CONTINUED)

PARAGUAY

1 January	New Year's Day
6 January	Epiphany
1 March	Heroes Day
Consult Calendar	Holy Thursday
Consult Calendar	Good Friday
1 May	Labor Day
14 - 15 May	Independence Day
12 June	Chaco Armistice
15 August	Founding of Asunción City
25 August	Constitution Day
29 September	Victory of Boquerón
12 October	Columbus Day
1 November	All Saints Day
8 December	Virgin of Cacupe
25 December	Christmas

PERU

1 January	New Year's Day
Consult Calendar	Holy Thursday
Consult Calendar	Good Friday
24 June	Countryman's Day
29 June	St. Peter and St. Paul's Day
28 July	Independence Day
29 July	National Day
20 August	St. Rosa of Lima Day
8 October	Navy Day
1 November	All Saints Day
8 December	Immaculate Conception
25 December	Christmas Day

SPAIN

1 January	New Year's Day
19 March	Feast of San José
Consult Calendar	Good Friday
Consult Calendar	Easter Sunday
1 May	Labor Day
24 June	The King's Birthday
25 June	Santiago Day
12 October	Columbus Day
1 November	All Saints Day
8 December	Immaculate Conception
25 December	Christmas

URUGUAY

1 January	New Year's Day
Consult Calendar	Holy Thursday
Consult Calendar	Good Friday
19 April	Landing of the 33 Patriots
1 May	Labor Day
18 July	Constitution Day
25 August	Independence Day
25 December	Christmas

APPENDIX D: HOLIDAYS (CONTINUED)

VENEZUELA

1 January	New Year's Day
Consult Calendar	Holy Thursday
Consult Calendar	Good Friday
19 April	Declaration of Independence Day
1 May	Labor Day
24 June	Battle of Carabobo
5 July	Independence Day
24 July	Simón Bolívar's Birthday
7 September	Public Officials' Day
12 October	Columbus Day
25 December	Christmas

APPENDIX E: STREET SIGNS

NO REBASE

NO PASSING

ANCHO LIBRE

HORIZONTAL CLEARANCE

PESO MAXIMO

MAXIMUM WEIGHT (METRIC TONS)

LIMITE

PARKING LIMIT

UNA HORA
8 a 21 h
DIAS HABILES

ONE-HOUR PARKING

NO

NO PARKING

NO

NO LEFT TURN

NO

NO RIGHT TURN

INSPECCION

INSPECTION

CONSERVE SU DERECHA

USE RIGHT LANE

MAXIMA

SPEED LIMIT (IN K.P.H.)

PEATONES A SU IZQUIERDA

PEDESTRIANS KEEP LEFT

ONE WAY

APPENDIX F: OTHER USEFUL SIGNS

PELIGRO	CUIDADO	PRECAUCION
DANGER	CAUTION	CAUTION

NO FUMAR	PROHIBIDO FUMAR	NO ENTRAR
NO SMOKING	NO SMOKING	DO NOT ENTER

ENTRADA	SALIDA	ABIERTO
ENTRANCE	EXIT	OPEN

CERRADO	VENTA	OFERTA
CLOSED	SALE	ON SALE

SE VENDE	PRECIO	DESCUENTO
FOR SALE	PRICE	DISCOUNT

SALA DE ESPERA	HORAS	HORARIO
WAITING ROOM	HOURS	HOURS

W.C.	BAÑO	HOMBRES
RESTROOM	RESTROOM	MEN

CABALLEROS	MUJERES	DAMAS
MEN	WOMEN	WOMEN

¡ATENCION!	LLAME	GRATIS
ATTENTION	CALL	FREE

ASCENSOR	ELEVADOR	BANCO
ELEVATOR	ELEVATOR	BANK

CASA DE CAMBIO	BOLETOS	INFORMACION
CURRENCY EXCHANGE	TICKETS	INFORMATION

PARADA	ESTACIONAMIENTO	FUERA DE SERVICIO
BUS STOP	PARKING LOT	OUT OF ORDER

ADUANA	**SERVICIO AL CLIENTE**	**POLICIA**
CUSTOMS	CUSTOMER SERVICE	POLICE

HORAS DE LLEGADA	**HORAS DE SALIDA**	**URGENCIAS**
SCHEDULE OF ARRIVALS	SCHEDULE OF DEPARTURES	EMERGENCY ROOM

CONSULTORIO	**HOSPITAL**	**TELEFONO**
DOCTOR'S OFFICE	HOSPITAL	TELEPHONE

BULEVAR	**CALLE**	**AVENIDA**
BOULEVARD	STREET	AVENUE

PLAZA	**JARDIN PUBLICO**	**CALLEJON SIN SALIDA**
SQUARE	PUBLIC GARDEN	DEAD END

PALACIO DE GOBIERNO	**PRIVADO**	**PARTICULAR**
CITY HALL	STAFF ONLY (PRIVATE)	STAFF ONLY (PRIVATE)

APPENDIX G: BASIC GEOGRAPHY

MEXICO

Mountains:
>   Sierra Madre Oriental
>   Sierra Madre Occidental

Cities **(see map)**:
>   Ciudad de México (Mexico City)
>   México, D.F. (also Mexico City)
>   Monterrey
>   Veracruz
>   Puebla
>   Guadalajara
>   Cancún
>   Mérida
>   Matamoros
>   Acapulco
>   San Luis Potosí
>   Ciudad Juárez

CENTRAL AMERICA AND THE CARIBBEAN (see map)

Countries and their Capitals:
>   Guatemala, Ciudad de Guatemala
>   (Guatemala City)
>   Honduras, Tegucigalpa
>   El Salvador, San Salvador
>   Nicaragua, Managua
>   Costa Rica, San José
>   Panamá, Ciudad de Panamá
>   (Panama City)
>   Cuba, La Habana (Havana)
>   República Dominicana
>   (Dominican Republic), Santo Domingo

SOUTH AMERICA

Mountains:
>   Los Andes

Rivers:
>   Río Amazonas (Amazon River)
>   Río Orinoco
>   Río Paraná
>   Río de la Plata

SOUTH AMERICA (Cont.)

Countries and their Capitals **(see map)**:
>   Colombia, Bogotá
>   Venezuela, Caracas
>   Ecuador, Quito
>   Chile, Santiago
>   Perú, Lima
>   Bolivia, La Paz
>   Paraguay, Asunción
>   Uruguay, Montevideo
>   Argentina, Buenos Aires

LATIN AMERICAN BODIES OF WATER

>   Gulf of Mexico
>   Caribbean Sea

SPAIN

Mountains:
>   Pirineos (Pyrenees)

Rivers:
>   Guadaquivir
>   Ebro
>   Duero

Cities **(see map)**:
>   Madrid
>   Bilbao
>   Sevilla
>   Barcelona
>   Toledo
>   Burgos
>   Zaragoza
>   Valencia
>   San Sebastián
>   Santander
>   Oviedo

Other Bodies of Water:
>   Bay of Biscay
>   Mediterranean Sea
>   Atlantic Ocean
>   Strait of Gibraltar

APPENDIX G: BASIC GEOGRAPHY (CONTINUED)

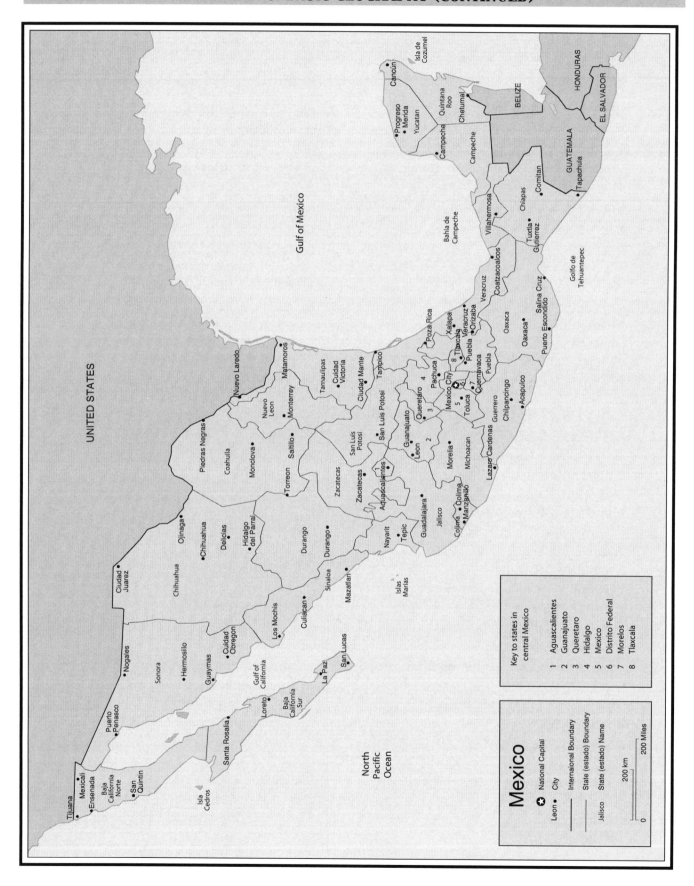

APPENDIX G: BASIC GEOGRAPHY (CONTINUED)

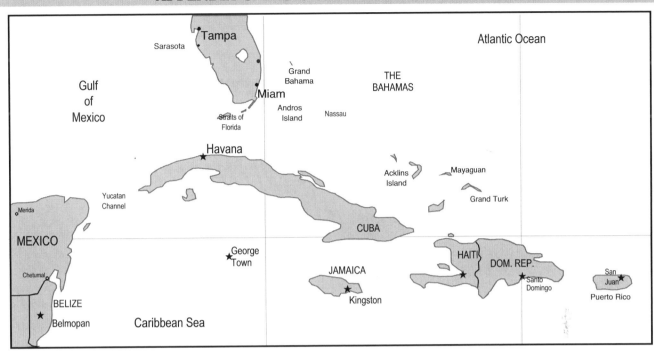

APPENDIX G: BASIC GEOGRAPHY (CONTINUED)

APPENDIX G: BASIC GEOGRAPHY (CONTINUED)

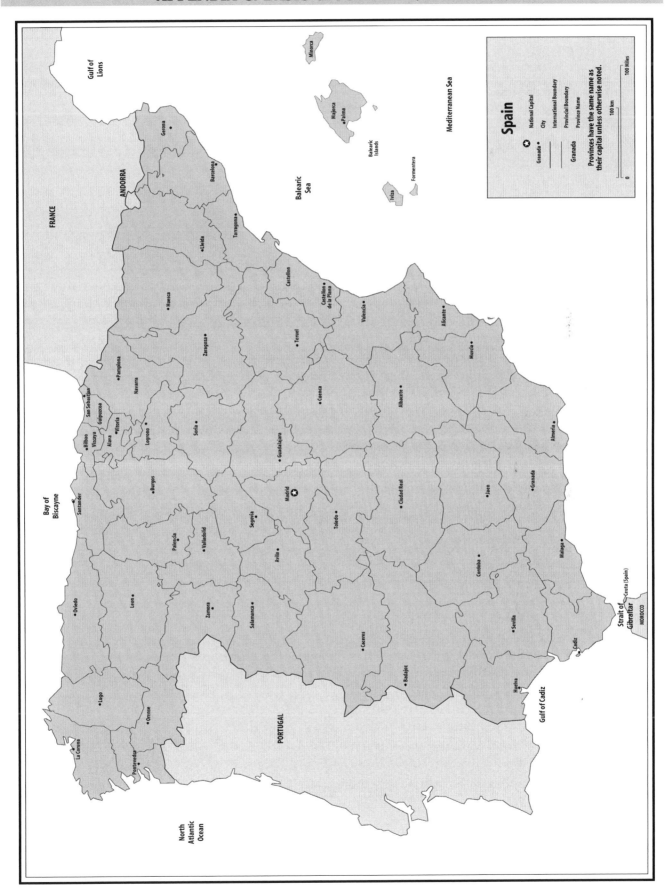

APPENDIX H: BASIC POLITICAL, SOCIAL, AND CULTURAL FACTS

ARGENTINA

Official Country Name: Argentine Republic

Population: 39,144,753

Capital: Buenos Aires

Monetary Unit: Argentine Peso

Major Cities: Buenos Aires, Córdoba, San Carlos de Bariloche, Comodoro Rivadavia, San Miguel de Tucumán, Mendoza

Religion: 92% Roman Catholic, 2% Protestant, 2% Jewish, 4% other

Area: 2,766,890 sq km (slightly more than four times the size of Texas or slightly less than three-tenths the size of the US)

Government: Republic made up of 23 provinces and one autonomous city. The president is elected for a term of 4 years. The bicameral National Congress, *Congreso Nacional*, is formed by the Senate and the Chamber of Deputies.

Economy: GDP 435.5 billion, $11,200 per capita

Labor Distribution: agriculture, industry, services.

Primary Exports: Edible oils, fuels and energy, cereals, feed, motor vehicles.

People: 97% white (Spanish and Italian) 3% Mestizo, Ameridian, and other.

Education: The literacy rate is 97.1%

Climate and Geography: The weather in general is mostly temperate, however, it is arid in the southeast, and sub-Antarctic in the southwest. Since Argentina is located in the southern hemisphere, the seasons are reversed; summer takes place December to March and winter is June to September. The average temperature from November to March is 23° C, and 12° C from June to September. Along the west, Argentina is bordered by the rugged Andes Mountains, the plains are located in the northern half of the country, and the plateau of Patagonia in the southern part. Argentina is home to the Aconcagua, South America's tallest mountain (6,960 m); Ushuaia , the southern most city in the world, and the Laguna del Carbón, the lowest point in the western hemisphere (-105m).

APPENDIX H: BASIC POLITICAL, SOCIAL, AND CULTURAL FACTS (CONTINUED)

ARGENTINA (continued)

Icons: Images about Argentina that first come to mind are tango music and dance style (musical expression of the Argentine soul); the Pampas plains and the gauchos (cowboys); Carlos Gardel (tango singer) and Evita Duarte de Perón. Significant thinkers and writers include Jorge Luis Borges (author, The Garden of Forking Paths), Julio Cortázar (author, *Hopscotch*), and Ernesto Sábato (author, *On Heroes and Tombs*). Noteworthy Argentines also include these Nobel Prize recipients: Carlos Saavedra Lamas (Peace, 1936); Bernardo Alberto Houssay, (Medicine, for hormone research, 1947); Adolfo Pérez Esquivel, (Peace, 1980); and César Milstein, (Medicine, for monoclonal antibodies research,1984).

Food and Drink: Beef is the key ingredient in the Argentine cuisine. *Parrillada mixta* (grilled meats) is found on almost every menu. Grilled meats are usually served with *chimichurri* sauce (oregano, garlic, parsley, spices, vinegar and oil). Other popular dishes include *matambre* (rolled stuffed flank steak), *empanadas* (turnovers) stuffed with chicken or beef, and *dulce de leche* (caramel). *Mate* tea is as common as coffee in the U.S. and is usually drunk from a gourd container. There are good Argentine wines, many from grapes grown at the foot of the Andes mountains. Among the best are the ones from the regions of Mendoza-Cuyo, Miapú, San Juan, San Rafael, and Uco Valley.

Sports and Leisure: Tennis, basketball, fishing, climbing and hiking, sailing, and skiing are widely practiced, however, soccer is the national sport. The Argentine national soccer team has won the World Cup twice (1978, 1986). Diego Armando Maradona is among the world's greatest soccer players. Gabriela Sabatini maintained her position in the tennis top ten ranking for a record of continuous 11 years (1985-1996).

Miscellaneous: Punctuality is relatively unimportant in Argentina, be prepared to wait for your counterpart. A handshake is the usual greeting in business and social gatherings. Measurements are given in the metric system. Argentina offers the visitor many natural attractions such as Iguazú Falls in the northeast (border with Brazil); the Pampas (in the center of the country), which is the largest area and best known for its grasslands and livestock activities; and the Patagonia region (to the south), with its forests and glaciers (especially impressive is the Perito Moreno Glacier). Among the sites recognized by the UNESCO World Heritage program are: the paintings at the Cave of the Hands, the Ischigualasto-Talampaya Natural Parks, the Jesuit Block and Estancias of Córdoba, and the Quebrada de Humahuaca –part of an Inca trail route. While in Buenos Aires visit the Metropolitan Cathedral, the Teatro Colón, the obelisk at Avenida Corrientes, and the old artists' quarter of La Boca, birthplace of the tango.

Travel: Although U. S. visitors may not need a visa to visit Argentina, it is recommended that you check with the Argentine Embassy in Washington D. C. prior to travel about current visa or permit requirements.

APPENDIX H: BASIC POLITICAL, SOCIAL, AND CULTURAL FACTS (CONTINUED)

COLOMBIA

Official Country Name: Republic of Colombia

Population: 44,185.775

Capital: Bogotá

Monetary Unit: Colombian Peso

Major Cities: Bogotá, Medellín, Cali, Barranquilla, Cartagena

Religion: 90% Roman Catholic

Area: 1,138,910 sq km (slightly less than three times the size of Montana)

Government: Republic composed of 32 departments and 1 capital district. The president is elected for a four-year term. The bicameral Congress, *Congreso*, consists of the Senate, *Senado*, and the House of Representatives, *Cámara de Representantes*.

Economy: GDP 263.2 billion, $6,300 per capita

Labor Distribution: 30% agriculture; 24% industry; 46% services.

Primary Exports: petroleum, coffee, coal, platinum, apparel, bananas, cut flowers.

People: 58% mestizo, 20% white, 14% mulatto, 4% black, 3% mixed black-Amerindian, 1% Amerindian.

Education: The literacy rate is 92.5%

Climate and Geography: Colombia is the only South American country that has a coastline both on the Caribbean Sea and the Pacific Ocean. The western side of the country is dominated by the Andes mountain range. The climate is tropical along the coasts and in the eastern plains, however the mountain ranges and highlands are considerably cooler. Colombia is one of the few places in the world with an Andean "Páramo" (high plateau region), characterized by a lack of trees, bunchgrass interspersed with shrub sedges, herbs, and low-lying mats of cushion plants, lichens, and mosses. Nearly 60 percent of all plant species found here grow nowhere else in the world. The Sierra Nevada range has perpetual snow on its highest peaks and it is located on the Caribbean Coast.

APPENDIX H: BASIC POLITICAL, SOCIAL, AND CULTURAL FACTS (CONTINUED)

COLOMBIA (continued)

Icons: Coffee, flowers, the Chibcha culture, and emeralds come to mind when speaking of Colombia. Noteworthy Colombians include Fernando Botero (painting), Gabriel García Márquez, Literature Nobel Prize recipient (1982, *One Hundred Years of Solitude*), John Leguízamo (comedian/actor), and Manuel Elkin Patarroyo (creator of the malaria vaccine). *Cumbia*, an African-based rhythm and dance, is the most popular folk type of music especially in the north of the country. It is characterized by loud bass drums and *millo* flutes playing while dancers in their bare feet move imitating the walk of long gone African slaves' whose feet were shackled together in chains.

Food and Drink: Any list of culinary Colombian delights must include *ajiaco* (chicken, corn and potato stew), *arroz con coco* (rice with coconut), *arepas* (white corn bread), *bandeja paisa* (a platter of red beans, rice, eggs, pork rinds, fried plantains, sausage, arepa, and ground beef), and *lechona* (stuffed pork with rice and ground meat). Coffee is the national drink. *Chicha*, is a drink made of corn. A popular drink in colder weather is *chocolate* (hot bitter cocoa with chunks of melting cheese inside). *Aguardiente* is an anis liquor. There are good wines from the Valle del Sol in Boyacá and Valle del Cauca.

Sports and Leisure: Some of the popular sports are cycling, baseball, scuba diving and other water sports, hiking and basketball, however the king of sports is soccer. Colombia was the champion at the Copa América Soccer Championship in 2001. Some of the most famous Colombian athletes are Lucho Herrera and Fabio Parra (cycling); Juan Pablo Montoya (Formula One driver); Carlos Valderrama, Faustino Asprilla (soccer), María Isabel Urrutia (weightlifting world champion), and Edgar Rentería and Orlando Cabrera (who represented the Red Sox and the Cardinals respectively during the World Series final in 2004 playing against each other).

Miscellaneous: Make appointments in advance. Punctuality is lax in Colombia; be prepared to wait for your counterpart. . A handshake is the usual greeting in business. Make sure you greet every single person in the room when arriving to a meeting as well as when leaving. Measurements are given in the metric system. If traveling to the highlands and Bogotá, you will need time to adjust to the high altitude. Some of the most famous festivals include the *Carnaval de Blancos y Negros* in Pasto, *Once de Noviembre* in Cartagena, Barranquilla's carnival, and *Feria de las Flores* in Medellín. The following are among the many sites recognized by the UNESCO World Heritage program: the Castillo de San Felipe de Barajas and fortress in Cartagena; Los Katíos National Park; the historic center of Santa Cruz de Mompox; the National Archeological Park of Tierradentro; and the San Agustín Archeological Park. While in the Bogotá area, visit the Gold Museum, *Monserrate* Cathedral at the top of a mountain, the historical neighborhood of *La Candelaria*, the Botanical Garden, and the Salt Cathedral and Mines of Zipaquirá.

Travel: U. S. visitors need a visa to visit Colombia. It is strongly recommended that you check with the Colombian Embassy in Washington D. C. prior to travel about current visa or permit requirements.

APPENDIX H: BASIC POLITICAL, SOCIAL, AND CULTURAL FACTS (CONTINUED)

COSTA RICA

Official Country Name: Republic of Costa Rica

Population: 3,956,507

Capital: San José

Monetary Unit: Costa Rican Colón

Major Cities: San José, Caldera, Puerto Limón, Puntarenas, Puerto Quepos

Religion: 73.6% Roman Catholic, 13.7% Evangelical, 1.3% Jehovah's Witnesses, 0.7% other Protestant, 4.8% other, 3.2% none

Area: 51,100 sq km (slightly smaller than West Virginia)

Government: Democratic republic formed by 7 provinces. The president is elected for a term of 4 years. There is a unicameral Legislative Assembly, *Asamblea Legislativa.*

Economy: GDP 35.34 billion, $9,100 per capita

Labor Distribution: 20% agriculture; 22% industry; 58% services.

Primary Exports: Coffee, bananas, sugar, pineapples, textiles, electronic components, medical equipment.

People: 94% white and meztizo; 3% black; 1% Amerindian; 1% Chinese, 1% other.

Education: The literacy rate is 96%

Climate and Geography: The weather is mostly warm as it is located in the tropics. The dry season lasts from December to April; the rainy season lasts from May to November. There are plains along the coasts, but the central part of the country is mountainous – including over 100 volcanoes.

Icons: Costa Rica is known as the land of volcanoes (some active like Volcán Arenas and Irazú). It is also unique in having no standing army. The *carreta costarricense* (typical ox-cart) is the national symbol. Another characteristic of Costa Rica is its rainforest where very highly venomous dart frogs (brightly colored tiny frogs) are found. Ex-President Oscar Arias was the recipient of the Nobel Peace Prize in1987. Alvaro Cardona-Hine is a well-known writer, painter and composer (*Frankenstein in Love*).

Food and Drink: Traditional dishes are based on staples of beef, chicken and fish dishes, with rice, corn or beans, and fresh fruit. Coffee is of very good quality and is the national drink.

APPENDIX H: BASIC POLITICAL, SOCIAL, AND CULTURAL FACTS (CONTINUED)

COSTA RICA (continued)

Sports and Leisure: Visitors may enjoy the many possibilities available: rafting, horseback riding, snorkeling, fishing, diving, kayaking, sport fishing, golf, bird watching, and surfing.

Miscellaneous: Make appointments in advance. Be on time for appointments. A handshake is the usual greeting and it is also used upon departure. Costa Rica is one of a handful of countries in the world that does not have an army. It was abolished in 1948. Costa Ricans believe in democracy and peace. Among the sites recognized by the UNESCO World Heritage program are: Talamanca Range-La Amistad Reserves / La Amistad National Park, Cocos Island National Park, and Area de Conservación Guanacaste. Canopy tours or tree top observation can provide you with a chance to explore up close the high-altitude ecosystems of the jungle and rain forest. There are sun-drenched beaches on the Pacific Ocean and on the Caribbean Sea.

Travel: Although U. S. visitors may not need a visa to visit Costa Rica, it is recommended that you check with the Costa Rican Embassy in Washington D. C. prior to travel about current visa or permit requirements.

MEXICO

Official Country Name: United Mexican States

Population: 104,959,594

Capital: Mexico City (*Distrito Federal*)

Monetary Unit: Mexican peso

Major Cities: Mexico city, Guadalajara, Monterrey, Oaxaca, Puebla, Querétaro, Morelia

Religion: Roman Catholic 89%, Protestant 6%, other 5%

Area: 1,972.550 sq km (slightly less than three times the size of Texas)

Government: Federal Republic composed of the Federal District and 31 states. The president is elected for a single six-year term. The bicameral Congress, *Congreso de la Unión*, consists of the Senate, *Cámara de Senadores*, and the Federal Chamber of Deputies, *Cámara Federal de Diputados*.

Economy: GDP 941.2 billion, $9,000 per capita

Labor Distribution: 18% agriculture; 24% industry; 58% services.

APPENDIX H: BASIC POLITICAL, SOCIAL, AND CULTURAL FACTS (CONTINUED)

MEXICO (continued)

Primary Exports: manufactured goods, oil and oil products, silver, fruits, vegetables, coffee and cotton.

People: 60% mestizo, 30% Amerindian, 9% white, 1% other

Education: The literacy rate is 92.2%

Climate and Geography: The climate varies from tropical in the low coastal plains and in the desert as well as in the high, rugged mountains, to temperate in the high plateaus (inland). Although enjoyable year-round, the best time to visit is between May and September to avoid the south's heat and humidity and the highlands' cold temperatures during December-February. The main mountain ranges are the Sierra Madre Occidental (along the west coast), the Sierra Madre Oriental (along the east coast) and the Transversal Volcanic System (along the 19° parallel from the Pacific to the Gulf of Mexico). The lowest point is the Laguna Salada (-10m), which contrasts with the Pico de Orizaba Volcano as the highest mountain at 5,700 m.

Icons: One of the world's major crops, corn, is thought to have originated in Mexico. Other images invoked when thinking of Mexico include tacos, the legacy of the Aztecs and Mayas, Pancho Villa, Emiliano Zapata, and even Chihuahua dogs. Significant Mexican thinkers, writers and artists include Octavio Paz (1990 Nobel Prize for Literature, *The Labyrinth of Solitude*), Carlos Fuentes (*The Death of Artemio Cruz, Old Gringo*), Amado Nervo (*At Peace*), Sor Juana Inés de la Cruz (*Poems, Protest, and a Dream*), Diego Rivera (muralist), Martha Chapa (painter and author), and Laura Esquivel (*Like Water for Chocolate*). Other influential Mexicans are Alfonso García Robles (Nobel Prize for Peace, 1982); Mario J. Molina (Nobel Prize in Chemistry, ozone studies, 1995); Luis Barragán (Pritzker Architecture Prize Laureate, 1980); architect Ricardo Legorreta Vilchis (International Union of Architects UIA Gold Medal, 1999); Alfonso Cuarón (director of *Harry Potter and the Prisoner of Azkaban*)

Food and Drink: A Mexican kitchen typically incorporates ingredients such as corn, cacti, chiles, cilantro, and tomato. Any list of culinary delights must include *tortillas* (flat corn or flour bread), *enchiladas* (rolled tortillas with chicken covered with a red or green sauce), *quesadillas* (folded tortillas with melted cheese inside), *cochinita pibil* (pulled pork meat), *ceviche* (fish marinated in lime juice), *machaca con huevos* (shredded meat jerky and eggs), *mixiotes de pollo* (seasoned chicken wrapped in maguey leaves). Typical beverages include *aguas frescas* (made of the fruit in season), *agua de jamaica* (hibiscus iced-tea), *horchata* (sweeten rice water) and hot chocolate. From succulents such as maguey, Mexicans obtain alcoholic drinks such as *tequila* (from blue agave), *pulque* (fermented not distilled), and *mezcal* (which is famous for having a worm in the bottle). Casa Madero, in northern Mexico, is the oldest winery in the Americas, founded in 1597. Also famous are the wines produced in Baja California. Mexican beer is world famous as well.

APPENDIX H: BASIC POLITICAL, SOCIAL, AND CULTURAL FACTS (CONTINUED)

MEXICO (continued)

Sports and Leisure: Sports like tennis, volleyball, cycling, basketball, martial arts, baseball and track are commonly practiced. Soccer is the most popular team sport, both to practice and as spectator sport. Hugo Sánchez Márquez, Alberto García Aspe, Carlos Manuel Hermosillo Goytortua, and Jorge Campos are some of the most famous soccer players in Mexico and abroad. Some of the sport activities available to travelers include mountain climbing, biking, hiking, diving, kayaking, golf, fishing, bird watching, and even whale watching (in the Baja Península).

Miscellaneous: Make appointments in advance. Punctuality is lax in Mexico; be prepared to wait for your counterpart. A handshake is the usual greeting in business. Measurements are given in the metric system. The following are among the many places recognized by the UNESCO as World Heritage Sites: the archaeological zones of Xochicalco, Paquimé, Calakmul, El Tajín, Monte Albán, Palenque, Chichen-Itzá, Teotihuacán, and Uxmal; the gardens of Xochimilco; the whale sanctuary of El Vizcaíno and the natural reserve of Sian Ka'an; the Franciscan missions in the Sierra Gorda of Querétaro; the historic centers of the cities of Puebla, Zacatecas, Campeche and Querétaro. The "clavadistas" (divers) are a great show to watch in Acapulco even at night. Major events and festivals happen almost every month, which include Carnaval (late February or early March), Día de los Muertos (November 2nd), and the Day of Our Lady of Guadalupe (December 12th). Acapulco and Cancún are world famous touristic cities and beaches.

Travel: Although U. S. visitors may not need a visa to visit Mexico, it is recommended that you check with the Mexican Embassy in Washington D. C. prior to travel about current visa or permit requirements.

PERU

Official Country Name: Republic of Peru.

Population: 27,544,305

Capital: Lima

Monetary Unit: Nuevo Sol

Major Cities: Lima, Iquitos, Trujillo, Paita, Yurimaguas, Huancayo

Religion: 90% Roman Catholic

Area: 1,285,220 sq km (slightly smaller than Alaska)

APPENDIX H: BASIC POLITICAL, SOCIAL, AND CULTURAL FACTS (CONTINUED)

PERU (continued)

Government: Constitutional republic made up of 24 departments and one constitutional province. The president is elected for a term of 5 years. There is a unicameral Congress of the Republic, *Congreso de la República del Perú.*

Economy: GDP 146 billion, $5,100 per capita

Labor Distribution: 5.9% agriculture; 0.4% mining and quarrying; 12.6% manufacturing; 5.3% construction, 26.3% commerce; 4.9% household work; 44.6% other services.

Primary Exports: fish and fish products, gold, copper, zinc, crude petroleum and by-products, lead, coffee, sugar, cotton.

People: 45% Amerindian, 37% mestizo, 15% white, 3% black, Japanese, Chinese and other.

Education: The literacy rate is 90.9%

Climate and Geography: Perú has tropical weather in the east; it is very dry on the west and extremely cold in the Andes. The rainy season is January to April, while the dry season is June to August. The west coast has flatlands, contrasting with the high and rugged mountains (Andes) in the center of the country, and the lowlands and jungle on the east. The Amazon River basin reaches the northeastern portion of the country. Huascará is the highest mountain at 6,770 m.

Icons: Images of the Andes, Incas, Cuzco, Machu Pichu, the Nazca lines, and llamas first come to mind when mentioning Peru. Significant Peruvian thinkers and writers include Mario Vargas Llosa (*The Time of the Hero*), José María Arguedas (*Deep Riversand*); Ciro Alegría (*The Golden Serpent*); César Vallejo (*Trilce*). Still popular is the Andean music with its indigenous instruments like the *kena* (bamboo flute), *zampoña* (panpipes), *ocarinas* (clay instruments), and drums made using hollow tree trunks and goatskin. One of the best known compositions of Andean music is *El Condor Pasa.*

Food and Drink: Key ingredients in Peruvian cuisine are the potatoes, yams and corn. The coast offers many seafood dishes like *cebiche* (lemon-marinated fish, served cold). An Inca specialty is roasted guinea pig. *Sopa a la criolla* (noodle soup with beef, vegetables and egg), *lomo saltado* (beef tenderloin, vegetables and rice dish), and *leche asada* (caramel) are popular and available in many restaurants. *Mate de coca* is an energy booster herbal tea. *Pisco* (Peruvian brandy) is used to prepare the mix drink: *pisco sour.* The best Peruvian wines come from the region of Ica.

Sports and Leisure: Although volleyball, tennis and rafting are commonly practiced sports, the most popular sport is soccer. Peru has been the champion twice at the Copa América in 1939 and 1975. Andes hiking is best during the dry season.

APPENDIX H: BASIC POLITICAL, SOCIAL, AND CULTURAL FACTS (CONTINUED)

PERU (continued)

Miscellaneous: Make appointments in advance. A handshake is the usual greeting and parting gesture in business and social gatherings. Punctuality is relatively unimportant; be prepared to wait. Measurements are given in the metric system. When traveling to any highlands area, be sure to leave time to adjust to the altitude. Some of the most famous Peruvian festivals are Carnaval, *Inti Raymi* (an Inca festival that takes place on June 24), and Puno Day in which people parade and dance wearing costumes. Arequipa, the "white city", offers the visitors colonial buildings made of volcanic rocks such as the Casa Ricketts and the Convento de Santa Catalina. Cuzco was the ancient Inca Empire capital and a "must visit" archeological site. Huaraz offers its permanently glaciated peaks and glacial lakes and hot springs. Isla Taquile is an island in Lake Titicaca , which is the world's highest navigable lake. Among the sites recognized by the UNESCO World Heritage program are: Chavin archaeological site, Chan Chán archaelogical zone, the historic downtown of Lima, and the historical downtown of Arequipa. Lima also offers the visitor the Gold Museum and the Textile Museum. The later houses examples of some of the oldest cloth in the western hemisphere.

Travel: Although U. S. visitors may not need a visa to visit Perú, it is recommended that you check with the Peruvian Embassy in Washington D. C. prior to travel about current visa or permit requirements.

SPAIN

Official Country Name: Kingdom of Spain

Population: 40,341,462

Capital: Madrid

Monetary Unit: Euro

Major Cities: Madrid, Barcelona, Valencia, Sevilla

Religion: 94% Roman Catholic, 6% other

Area: 504,782 sq km (slightly more than twice the size of Oregon)

Government: Parliamentary monarchy made up of 17 autonomous communities and two autonomous cities. The president is elected for a term of 4 years. The bicameral National Assembly, *Corte General*, is formed by the Senate, *Senado*, and the Congress of Deputies, *Congreso de los Diputados*.

Economy: GDP 937.6 billion, $23,300 per capita

APPENDIX H: BASIC POLITICAL, SOCIAL, AND CULTURAL FACTS (CONTINUED)

SPAIN (continued)

Labor Distribution: 5.3% agriculture; 30.1% manufacturing; mining and construction; 64.6% services.

Primary Exports: machinery, motor vehicles, foodstuffs, pharmaceuticals, medicines, other consumer goods.

People: Basques, Catalans, Galicians, (regional language groups), Moroccans, and South Americans (primary immigrant groups)

Education: The literacy rate is 98.7%

Climate and Geography: Usually hot summers especially in the high central plains. Spain is the second most mountainous country in Europe, ringed by various mountain chains: the Pyrenees along the French border, The Sierra Nevada in the South and East, the Guadarrama in the North Central and the Cantabrian, along the Northern coast. The Canary Islands (off the coast of Africa) and the Balearic Islands (in the Mediterranean) are also part of Spain. The highest mountain is Pico de Teide on the Canary Islands.

Icons: Cervantes' Don Quixote; bullfighting and the toreador; Velázquez' *Las Meninas*, flamenco music and dance, the guitar, and Picasso's cubism are just a few of Spain's representative images. Significant Spanish thinkers and writers include Miguel de Cervantes Saavedra (*Don Quijote*), and the following Nobel Literature Laureates: José Echegary (*The Avenger's Wife*,1901), Juan Ramón Jiménez (*Diary of a Newly-Wed Poet*, 1956), Vicente Aleixandre (*The Shadow of Paradise*, 1977), and Camilo José Cela (*Mrs. Caldwell talks with her son*, 1989). Other influential Spaniards are Santiago Ramón y Cajal, 1906 Nobel Prize for Medicine (nervous system studies); Severo Ochoa 1959 Nobel Prize for Medicine (nucleic acid); Joan Miró (painter), Salvador Dalí (painter), El Greco (painter), Federico García Lorca (author of *Blood Wedding*), Miguel de Unamuno (author of *Cancionero*), Antonio Gades (dancer), Andrés Segovia (guitarrist), Julio Iglesias (singer), Antonio Banderas and Penélope Cruz (actors), and Pedro Almodóvar (film director, 1999 Oscar® for *All About My Mother*).

Food and Drink: Traditional Spanish dishes include: *fabada* (haricot bean stew), *tortilla española* (Spanish omelet with potatoes), *paella valenciana* (saffron rice mixed shell-fish, and/or chicken), *jamón serrano* (cured ham), *bacalao a la vizcaína* (cod), *patatas bravas* (spiced potatoes), *pollo a la chilindrón* (chicken fried covered with a ham sauce), *cochinillo a la segoviana* (roasted pig), *chorizo* (Spanish sausage), and *gazpacho* (cold raw vegetable soup). A popular drink is *sangría* (wine punch). Spain is famous for having good wines, among the best are those from the regions of Catalonia, La Rioja, Galicia, and Castilla-León; sherry comes from the Andalucían province of Jerez.

APPENDIX H: BASIC POLITICAL, SOCIAL, AND CULTURAL FACTS (CONTINUED)

SPAIN (continued)

Sports and Leisure: Sports like tennis, basketball, cycling, golf, handball, and beach soccer, are widely practiced, however the most popular sport is soccer (to play and to watch). Another popular spectator sport is Formula One racing. Outstanding Spanish athletes include Arantxa Sánchez Vicario (tennis), Conchita Martínez (tennis), Sergio García (golf), Fernando Alonso (Formula One racing), Emilio Butragueño Santos (soccer), Iker Casillas Fernández (soccer), Raúl González Blanco (soccer), and Carles Puyol (soccer).

Miscellaneous: Make appointments well in advance. Unless you are attending a bullfight, you may need to wait for your counterpart to arrive. A handshake is the usual greeting in business and social gatherings. Spain is a member of the European Union. Measurements are given in the metric system. Among the sites recognized by the UNESCO World Heritage program are: Altamira cave and its prehistoric paintings, the Roman walls of Lugo, the Alhambra, Generalife (in Granada), the old town of Segovia and its aqueduct, the university and historic precinct of Alcalá de Henares, the pilgrimage route to Santiago de Compostela, and the historic centers of the cities of Córdoba, Santiago de Compostela, and Cáceres. Some of Madrid's landmarks include the Prado Museum, the Centro de Arte Reina Sofía National Museum, Puerta del Sol, Puerta de Alcalá, and Buen Retiro Park. Some of the attractions of Barcelona include Palau de la Música Catalana (music hall), Picasso Museum, Gaudí Museum and Home, Miró Foundation, the demonstrations of the Castellers (impressive human towers), and its Mediterranean beaches.

Travel: Although U. S. visitors may not need a visa to visit Spain, it is recommended that you check with the Spanish Embassy in Washington D. C. prior to travel about current visa or permit requirements.

To order this title and/or other titles…

You may photocopy or remove the order form found on the reverse side and return it to us OR you may phone us toll free at 1-800-931-5264 to order any of the following titles:

- *Basic French for Travelers*

- *Basic German for Travelers*

- *Basic Italian for Travelers*

- *Basic Japanese for Travelers*

- *Basic Portuguese for Travelers*

- *Basic Spanish for Travelers*

Not ordering?

That's okay. We still want to know what you think of this manual. Please complete the bottom portion of the reverse side of this page and return it to us.

Language 911

PRODUCT ORDER FORM

Order additional copies of this book, or any other Language 911® product listed below, using this form.

SHIP TO:

Name:

Company:

Street Address (no PO Boxes):

City: State: Zip:

Telephone: (   )

METHOD OF PAYMENT [NO CHECKS]:

☐ Money Order (enclosed)   ☐ VISA   ☐ MasterCard

Card Number:

Expiration Date:

Name (as on card):

Signature:

Item	Title	Unit Price	Quantity	Total
BFT	*Basic French for Travelers*	$19.95		
BGT	*Basic German for Travelers*	$19.95		
BIT	*Basic Italian for Travelers*	$19.95		
BJT	*Basic Japanese for Travelers*	$19.95		
BPT	*Basic Portuguese for Travelers*	$19.95		
BST	*Basic Spanish for Travelers*	$19.95		

Total Price

(see note at right) **Shipping/Handling**

(U.S. Funds only) **TOTAL**

SHIPPING/HANDLING
(for Continental U.S. delivery)

FOR GROUND DELIVERY

Quantity Ordered	Commercial Delivery	Residential Delivery
1-15	$5.60	$7.60
16+	35¢ ea.	55¢ ea.

For faster delivery options, please phone 1-800-931-5264 for shipping fees.

If you are ordering more than 50 of the same title, you may be eligible for a discount. Call for more information.

FAX:
601-582-5177

MAIL:
Language 911®
PO Box 1091
Petal, MS 39465

PHONE:
1-800-931-5264

TAKE 2 MINUTES TO GIVE US YOUR 2 CENTS
...even if you aren't placing an order.

Product Title?_____

Where did you purchase this product?_____

Did you find this book helpful?   ☐ Very   ☐ Somewhat   ☐ Not at all

Did we leave anything out?_____

_____

Would you like to receive notices of updated materials?   ☐ Yes   ☐ No

If yes, what's your e-mail?_____